a bus

a bus stop

a lorry

a milk lorry

a car

a police car

a big bus

a big bus
and
a big lorry
and a car

a little lorry
and a big car

a big lorry
and a little car

the lorry driver
and the bus driver

the bus driver is
in the bus.

the lorry driver is
in the lorry.

a shop
the shop is a paper shop.

the big lorry is
at the paper shop.

the driver is
in the shop.

a big shop
and a little shop

the car is
at the little shop.

a police car

a big police car
and
a big policeman

the driver is
in the police car.

the driver is
a policewoman.

the bus is going
to Hill Street.

the paper shop is
in Hill Street.

the bus is
at the bus stop.

the driver is reading
a paper.

the police car is
in Hill Street.

the driver is
at the big shop.

the milk lorry is
in Hill Street.

the driver is going
to the little shop.

the bus is in Hill Street.
the car is at a shop.
the policeman is
in the car.
the lorry is
at the bus stop.
the driver is going
to a shop.